BEWARE OF OLDER MEN

Also by Merrit Malloy

THINGS I MEANT TO SAY TO YOU WHEN WE WERE OLD

MY SONG FOR HIM WHO NEVER SANG TO ME

Merrit Malloy

BEWARE
OF
OLDER MEN

A DOLPHIN BOOK

Doubleday & Company, Inc.
Garden City, New York
1980

Library of Congress Catalog Card Number 79–6886
ISBN: 0-385-15942-0

First Edition

This book is for those of us who still cry in movies
and laugh in bed . . .

For those with hidden wings . . .

And especially . . .

For CINDY BADHAM: Who harvests songs in children.

For ERNESTYNE WHITE: That dear lamb who broke from the
fold—Who celebrates the signing of any Independence.

For DIANA LEVINE: My pal . . . who has a thousand hearts.

For ANNE PHILLIPS: Who left with my old Volkswagen key.

For DAVID: Who has the courage to care out loud.

For MARY McDONNELL: For the Chesapeake summers of my
discontent.

For CHUCK MORRELL: That champion.

For MOLLY MALLOY: That Irish poet . . . That sweet canvas
. . . That swan.

For THE SAILOR I saw in the woods when I was nine years old.

For PETE and GRACIE: Who had their fur loved off . . . Who
can never die . . .

For JOLENE WOLFF: A gypsy moth . . . My cherished friend
. . . The lady.

For MAC: That restless seed . . . That Fancy Dancer . . .
That magician.

For PETER MALLOY: Because he taught me how to tie my shoes.

For MARILYN PETERSON: My splendid friend . . . who knows
why.

For SUZANNE: Because she was always a beauty.

For LINDY HESS: My editor . . . who looked the other way and
let me steal a few bases.

For TALLY MALLOY—Because it matters.

For JANIS IAN: Who has majesty . . . Whose splendid gifts

have underlined the truth and whose songs will celebrate the air in every room I ever live in . . .

For HELEN MALLOY: Who taught me how to make love from scratch.

For THE BAG LADY in New York who sold me a rainbow for a dollar.

For CHARLIE: Because he was a sucker for a sad song . . . Because of the Rose Garden . . . Because . . .

For MY GOODTIME PALS: Barbara, Shauna, Bill, Jason, George the Nick, Stephen, Donald, Ringer . . . and THE GANG THAT COULDN'T SING STRAIGHT . . .

And mostly . . .

For LEE PHILIPS, THE MAN WHOSE FATHER READ BOOKS: Because he is a renegade . . . Because he's determined to remain available for miracles . . . Because he brought me O'Casey . . . Because he never went to camp . . . Because the rich ARE different . . . and Because We Ain't Seen Nothin' yet! . . . And . . .

For MONASH: That giant love . . . Because he WAS a free man in Paris . . . Because he rejoiced in my flights . . . Because he slayed the dragons . . . Danced with the children and brought me to the sea . . .

And finally . . .

For YOU: The bunch of you . . . Who I may never know . . . It's for that part of you that comes to these pages . . . That locks in a common memory . . . It's for that simple bullseye that every writer prays for . . . Because when everything else has been said . . . That's the only connection that remains . . . And the only inheritance I came to leave.

MERRIT MALLOY
August 1979
Malibu, California

A NOTE FROM THE AUTHOR

This book has no traditional design—
a pattern that may bridge in sections . . . and
separate the skin—
It came in pieces—unrehearsed—
No one page ends to begin another—
there are no final prayers or
winners—

I can only hope that you don't
look for logic here—and
that you are among those who
need no explanation—

Because

I have none—

BEWARE OF OLDER MEN

I can only promise you this . . .

. . . What I write may not be true

But . . . It's not a lie . . .

THE BOOK
I SAID I'D NEVER WRITE

This is the book I said I'd never write
. . . The book you saw in print
When you called my gifts 'fatal'
. . . When all the seeds in me
Were still beneath the ground . . .

And I prayed that you were wrong
. . . I prayed that freedom
Would not capture me
. . . That I would never leave
Your house
. . . Or breathe outside your arms . . .

You called them 'baby pictures' . . . My first books
Old neighborhoods
Where I could say that I grew up
. . . 'Word paintings'
The finger flesh I used to earn your Father love . . .

It was you who saw him coming
. . . Like the first images of a Polaroid
'He is closer by miles than inches' you wrote
Closer by miles
. . . Than inches . . .

And I prayed that you were wrong
. . . I never dreamed that you'd be left

In the rooms where I loved you
. . . Closer to me by miles
Than inches
. . . Left to read a book like this
The book I said I'd never write . . .

I thought that I could love them both . . .
That too many answers wouldn't change the question . . .
I didn't know that memory divides . . .
Slices every morning right in half . . .
I'd forgotten that the rich go mad
From too many alternatives . . .
I didn't plan to love them both
. . . split the ticket
And be left like this . . .
To choose the better man . . .

I'd rather die myself . . . The Mother cried
. . . I'd rather die than choose between the two
Or kill them both
As another woman might
To not be left with one alive
and one child dead . . .

I thought that I could love them both
. . . That I could choose not to make a choice
I didn't know that it would come to this

. . . where the highway divides
and runs off the pages of the maps
I didn't plan to love them both
To be cursed with too much love and not too little
. . . No one ever taught me
How to beg for less . . .

His hands came across the table
. . . one at a time . . .
They formed a cradle around my fingers
. . . and squeezed a reassurance . . .
I felt ashamed
. . . And the lids came down upon my eyes
He squeezed again . . . more sad this time
                                  than friendly . . .
I wondered if he knew . . .

Last night he closed the gates at the entrance
                                  to our home . . .
. . . He closed the lights that always guide the pathway
                                  to our door . . .
And he turned the lock from the inside . . .
Forcing me to ring the bell . . . Like a common stranger
Forced to raise the house awake
Attention toward the clock I hung myself
. . . I wondered now how much he knew
How long . . . and

His body rushed so selfishly . . .
Uncommonly direct
. . . He took me with a native right
As men less kind or strangers might
. . . I felt abuse and pain
But not my own . . .
And I crawled on my knees across the battlefield
                                  . . . those flowered sheets
I snuggled in against the heat that seemed more sad
                                  than angry now . . .

I offered my hand . . . prepared to be refused
                                    an entrance now
. . . And all of me was taken in . . . Forgiven
                              and brought back alive
As I thought about the other man whose hands
                              came across the table
. . . No more than an hour ago . . . One at a time . . .
I felt ashamed . . .
And the lids came down upon my eyes . . .
I wondered if *he* knew . . .

BEWARE OF OLDER MEN

He was not the first
. . . There had been many before him
All of them had classic lines
Mostly . . . the hair had whitened
Each had tennis shorts . . . (some had courts)
All of them were cured of youth—
Each believed in resurrection
a time ahead—reduced
a future from the past
. . . I was their folly . . .
I was their disease
. . . All of them had style
Each had the humanity of time lost
Mostly . . . they held hands . . .
. . . There were many
He was not the first . . .

It began as a fantasy . . .
She was a writer . . . a fledgling
reckless in the way he used to be
when he was going to change the world
. . . the same world
before she was born . . .

It was a pursuit of innocence
. . . In him she looked for the grace
That younger men were denied with women
That appreciation of light/design

There was a quality in the fabric of his flesh
. . . He was a grown-up . . .

And he adored her . . .
She was hopeful
. . . She had childhood flesh
She applauded his lechery/honored his honest need
. . . She allowed him entrance into her body/he brought
the harvest

She defended his death
With her life . . .
. . . She was a bargain . . .

She knew the first moment she saw him
. . . No, not his name . . . Even though within months
It would be her name . . .
She knew that he had what she needed . . . And
she knew that he would need
what she had . . .
Yes . . . There was exchange . . . But
Mostly . . . it was love . . .

She was uneasy with him . . .
He would use that if he had to . . .
. . . he was a marksman . . . she was prey
His confidence was born of her insecurity
It was a mutual child . . .

What he took from her was the need
To take care of herself . . .
What she took from him was the need
To find someone like *her* . . .
It didn't take an expert
To trace this core of discontent
. . . When the answers arrived
She knew the questions.

It began years before
She walked with a man in a rose garden
He loved her more than anything on Earth
He would take care of her
He would never leave . . .
A year later he was dead . . . she was six years old
. . . He was her Father

And now she was in the rose garden again
Turning strangers into heirlooms
. . . When she cried
She only cried for more . . .
He would take care of her
He would never leave . . .
A year later he was gone
She was twenty-eight years old
. . . He wasn't her Father

Oh no, it wasn't that way at all
. . . it wasn't
And there is no way to tell you
. . . No perfect metaphor

You see . . .
She was a believer
. . . She had faith
Three glasses of wine and
The truth became
Theory again . . .
. . . She could change her past
To fit the present
. . . She was a believer

And when they were married
. . . they were both the same age/they loved each other
The clichés were all corrupted
. . . They had it all
(And for all they knew
. . . That was all there was)

She was a writer
. . . born that way
He was a producer
(no, it wasn't that simple)
He was a writer too
Neither one ever did anything on purpose
That they didn't do
By accident first . . .
It was an even exchange
He was not the first

Before long . . .
He had taken her from those small rooms where
she wrote books . . . To
great white houses

. . . To the sea
. . . To larger rooms . . .
She had a lot of paper now
Mighty black electric typewriters
. . . it was not her native soil
But she was well received
. . . She was his lady . . .
(who also wrote little books
and fostered children . . .)

Soon . . . She was another of his children
Another of his wives
Another of his assets
Another of
his credits
. . . debits . . . She was not the first.

And he . . .
He was resident among the others now
He had the classic lines
Another of her lovers/another of her Fathers
Another death her life survived . . .

And then they say
She took a lover on the side
. . . went the way of younger women
Except that she went further
. . . Loved her lover
Turned thirty
And
Healed her age with larger books

More splendid men
. . . (I know what you're thinking
But you're wrong) . . .

He came to the net
And isn't that the trump
For the girl who can't play games . . .
Their leaving had no moderation
. . . They bled on each other
Dirtied the dream
Made no sense of freedom . . .
In the end . . . Each was robbed a little
Of what the other was rich in . . . (So they say)

Yes, both of them still eat apples
They don't drive past the old house anymore
. . . It's just a house
Both had a lot of those
Too many . . . I suspect

They were finally reduced
To former roommates
. . . Legal papers littered the quilted tablecloth
Her Mother handmade . . .
Each was left with severance pay
. . . a portion of the other's talent
These are the marbles
(the aggie's he called them)
. . . He didn't really mean it.

They have used their guilt well
. . . They have disguised their hatred as pain

Disguised their pain as hatred . . .
Common punishments . . . Petty thefts
Dollar bills have paper hearts
Ironically . . . Each had a lot of money then
What they held out for
Was love . . .
(they didn't get enough)
Christmas will be hard this year.

*

And yes . . .
I beware of older men
. . . I am frightened of how little they want

. . . I am weary of my fine silks.
I am a cynic now in these great white houses
My faith has retreated to myself
I no longer look for absolution—And
. . . I am terrified of gifts

The question is not in the answer anymore
. . . And it continues
The payments still to come . . .
The profits negotiable . . .

He used me brilliantly
To increase his life
And I used him brilliantly
To kill my Father
. . . Finally
Where there were many for both of us . . . Now
There are none . . .
He was the last . . .

But it was never like that at all
. . . I promise you these legal dances are further lies
And we came together to cure the need for redemption.
. . . No matter what you hear
Love cannot be reduced with orders that show cause
. . . Love is the cause
It is the only thing that stays
. . . It is not an even exchange
And
It is not equitable . . .

They say we were married . . .
That I was looking for a Father
That he was looking toward my public flesh
But . . . Stop them . . . If you hear them . . . Please
Because . . .
We loved each other once . . .
We held hands . . .
We understood the meaning of time
And
Even then . . .
We knew this would come. . . .
These are payments now
Too high for the bargains we once thought ourselves
But worth it . . . I would say . . .
(Oh, that word again)
Equitable

Trust is an offering, I think . . .
It has more to do with faith than love
And . . . it is more sacred . . .

And I'll ask you for it now
. . . It must be taken or left
Not stuck in committee
. . . Not filed under "M"
. . . Not scratching hopelessly in the air.

We are not two bodies anymore
Not bulging cock
. . . Not milk-fed thighs
We have redeemed our
pornography . . . And

You are free to anything I have
that can be counterfeit
. . . Anything that can be replaced
Reduced to currency
. . . Or explained . . . But

Trust is an offering, I think
It cannot be extorted
There are no counter offers
. . . I'll ask you for it now

. . . Beware

THEORY

If I had met you at ten
you might have pinched my cheeks
sniffing for my mama's favors
And . . . I would have thought you one of them
A Mother stealer
or worse . . . A male adult
A part vacated by my Father
or the coming enemy
who thought in other languages.

Thirty years my senior . . .
. . . We would have been an awkward pair . . .
At fifteen . . . Had I met you . . . vegetarian hitchhiker
                                    deluxe/freckled wisdom
I might have attacked your philosophy
excavating for my own . . . or . . . You may have been
                                    a surrogate Charlie . . .
I may have followed you and called you Christ . . .
Eaten you alive . . .
A year later . . . or before
You would yield to my seduction . . . Pay the
                                    first class fare
. . . And you'd miss the subtle colors . . .
It was at Seventeen
When I first canceled the light parades . . .
                                    a historical event for me . . .
It was that year exactly . . . That I chose
                                    to be a double agent . . .

It was the year I played woman . . .
The year my family called my life

                                    a critical success . . .
If I had met you then . . . You might have seen

                                    a fair first draft
. . . You might have seen the promise . . .
But I was suspect then . . . especially of male adults
. . . Thirty years my senior?
I might have been a common cliché and

                                    you might not object . . .
. . . Surely there would be exchange . . . uneven volume

                                    in our prayers
. . . At Seventeen . . . I could not have known you well

                                    or long . . . And
we might have wasted more than time

                                    lost in our translations . . .
And if I'd seen you on the streets locked in your

                                    expensive cars . . .
You may not have seen the aristocracy in my bare feet
that you see today
That wasn't there at all.

And Vietnam ran parallel to my pregnancies
Both were conflicts I fought not to fight
As a child Mother . . .
You might have seen my huge milk breasts
overlooking my backpack babies
But you would have found me far too old at twenty-one
Out of things to dream so soon

My spirit hardly caught a thermal through that time . . .
                    And you might have found me dull indeed
Sparrows are so hard to see
And I could not have heard you for the noise . . .

You only could have been a surface scratch
on my thick skin at twenty-two . . .
                                I was closed for repairs
Grieving for myself through martyred kings
All my pain had to be for something?
I may have made you my cause
And my effect
Or I may have tortured you perversely in payment
for loving me
when I could not love myself

It was only then
in those few moments at Fox
Only then when we had the perfect rite of passage
A year before . . . I would have stopped you at the gate
You might have made me one of many
just six months before
But we cut through all the tissue
                                with those first shots
skipped all the elementary grades
It was a chance we had to take without notice . . .
                                an emergency union
The least expected of miracles one might find
                                in a commissary line
At twenty-six . . . I was both old enough to see you
                    and young enough to be seen

I wondered . . . all that afternoon
how we could have missed each other
                              within the boundaries of that lot
Within the glass displays of those square miles
How we must have been on the same floors
                              in the same buildings
How we might have been
introduced and forgotten more than once
But it might be true . . . That people brought together
                              too soon

or too late
might be dismissed politely . . . Overlooked
You may have come so close I couldn't focus
I may have been with another man
And you . . .
with another woman
Just content enough to be free of discontentment
And I loved you in those days with every muscle I had
You were in every frame
And no one ever cherished me with quite the same
                              velocity
You did . . . You know . . . Love me up at every age
                              and angle
No one would believe the celebration . . . Not
                    and still believe that we survived . . .

And if I had met you now . . . This afternoon . . .
Surely I would love you twice . . . and all at once again
But how differently we might approach the threshold now
In my thirtieth summer . . . I'm more protective of
                              the sun

more careful now than then to send my courage blind
                              toward some Columbus
Discrimination is a word used by closet cowards . . .
                                        I suppose
And I don't know how it might be for you
                              to come upon me now
with all my silks and expensive friends.

You . . . The man in you evolved so far
how supremely simple it became this year
the clear clean patience that charms you even more
Could you look at me today?
With all this sophistication sewn so cleverly
                                        through out
Could you cure me now of these obscure ambitions?
Would you love me here . . . wrapped in
                              typewriter ribbons
Unavailable to wear to parties
Or to be touched at all sometimes . . . Like now
When the words become dictator
Could you still love a girl who dreams too high
                              and sleeps too late
Could you murder these careers? . . . Could you
                              love me now
Even though I've jumped the fence
Bucked you off and . . . could you watch me pursue
                              innocence and independence
knowing that I may not be among the mourners?
Can you love me with the same vulnerability now
                    that you know I'm a sprint runner
A quarter horse

A sugar high?

How could you love me now??? . . . Thirty years my senior
Having been this road
Having seen this film so many times before???
. . . It's two o'clock . . . A little early for these

late promises

But with all the changing of the guard
All the revolutions past and present
With all these thirty summers accumulated
With everything I know that's true
That changes and may not stay true . . . For all the

other times

I loved you then
these past four years with colors I may never use

again

I loved you then with a child's faith . . . And
I loved you far more often
But . . . I know this much . . . *I've loved you better*
. . . But *I've never loved you more* . . .

I COULDN'T SAY IT THEN

I couldn't say it then
or ever—
I had lost the understanding
of words—But

Whole landscapes of my memory
were reassembled
the day Paul left—
The roots beneath me hardened
—I could no longer remember
my mother's face—
So I didn't try and charm him
review his glory
or indict him for doing
what he had to
to stay alive—
We had put an animal to sleep once
the two of us—our good Easter manners had been useless
—We knew the enemy—

I could say that our hearts were broken
But it was more critical than that
the pain so primal
a wrong move
might cause paralysis—
and I could not comfort him
—I was what he suffered from

So I could not say it then
or ever
How could I explain
the naked force of knowing
that I would always see him leaving
and
that the sight of it
would always
Bring him back?

Don't you dare put your arms around me
As though you were a family friend
. . . As though you weren't one of the two men
Eclipsing my life . . . Don't
You dare . . .

Relax . . . I'm not going to die
I'm only going to wish I had
. . . The terrible thing is that I will become
Indifferent . . .
I won't even care enough
Not to care . . .
. . . In time
There will just be air
. . . air

So please don't be the eager volunteer
Who shows up when all the work is done
. . . anxious to contribute everything you can
After the election . . . Please
Don't you dare
Say you love me . . . Don't
You dare . . .

EARLY MOURNING FOR PAUL

It is now Tuesday morning (2 A.M.)
Late Monday night
. . . Again
A matter of interpretation . . .

I feel . . . here at this typewriter
That I am both the cause
And the effect
Of this late night isolation . . .
(self-imposed)
This is not an unfamiliar place for me . . .

It is as though I am writing this from far away
(And perhaps, I am . . .)
The distance is deliberate
I think we have suffered each other more now
. . . Reduced to paper greetings

Soon we will both become books
. . . We will be reviewed in dinner conversation
We will have profit
Even in the leaving—oh,
. . . There is no stopping success

I am beaten with the thought
Of these unfriendly days . . .
The weight of it
. . . The sadness

I feel I will have to excavate the original designs
Find the source of us and
Bear it out
With deep breathing
. . . Mind tricks . . .

There are wild cards further
. . . Perhaps there is a God
As the sisters promised
. . . Perhaps these legal strangers will mislead us
Perhaps . . .

It is now Tuesday morning . . . (2 A.M.)
Or late Monday night
. . . Again
A matter of interpretation . . .
Leaving has no moderation
. . . We come hard
We leave harder . . .

Like you
. . . I bless these wings
My memory is still breathing . . .

Anger falls hard
Like anchor rope
On the stern of your chin
. . . And
I hold my breath
As a baby holds her breath
Hanging in the air

Above her Father
Trusting him to catch her . . .

But you do not break the fall
. . . You let me slam down on your heart
And fall unloved
To the ground . . .

Leaving has no moderation . . .

And you will come down harder still
Force my breath from its double home
. . . And finally I know . . .

That you have cheated on this final exam . . .
You have stolen money from your Mother's purse

· And this is the inconsolable . . .
. . . The last sacrament
Membership to hell
These are
. . . The Northern scars . . .

Leaving has no moderation . . .

LOVE AMONG THE RUINS

We are near the finish line now
. . . A good night's sleep
And we can rewrite these
Bad metaphors . . .
. . . Revise the motives

My eyes will always refuse
the knowledge of you in other arms . . .
I will always see you in mine
When we were journeymen lovers
And God
Was smiling . . .

The design is cruel
. . . To die alive
Not to see the bodies lowered
. . . To know the beloved
Will not wait for you in heaven
. . . Or even call . . .

The results are almost in
. . . There were some far regions in the heart
still unaccounted for . . .
Soon the commentators on all three channels
Will agree
. . . The computers always know first
And still I always hope
A block of votes

Could mend this science
. . . Insult these arrogant predictions

It is almost over
. . . The scars are welcome cover
The skin has not stopped . . .
. . . The body is a love
Among these ruins
. . . And this sadness is testimony
To the life in this soil . . .

It came from love
. . . this loss
And because it was a beauty
We have that further indignity
A double
Amputation . . .
A brutal surgery
for that
Innocence . . .

I write/dripping from the pen
My mind's saliva
. . . My life is red and sore
We are maimed/consumed by change
The tracings dissolved . . .

I want to throw up a crucifix
To stop the law
. . . To protect young lovers
From this statistic

. . . To see
God smile . . .

But . . .
We are almost there
. . . A good night's sleep
And we can revise this violence
As a new Mother revises her labor pains
. . . We can rewrite
These bad metaphors
. . . Reconstruct this outline
To fit the final drafts . . .

In time . . .
The human will coagulate a kindness
The original wood
Is still there
. . . Change is not final
It is constant
. . . And this sadness
Is testimony
To the life
. . . In this soil . . .

So squeeze away this image
Postdate these checks
. . . And get a good night's sleep
The skin
Has not stopped . . .

RITES OF PASSAGE

There was a moment
. . . No more than that
When you walked through
The room and turned
. . . You didn't say it . . . No
. . . But the rites of passage
Are narrow
And come just once
. . . If you hadn't left
That morning
. . . Before breakfast
You would have stayed
For the rest
Of your life . . .

THE LATE NEWS

No, clearly I have been the jerk . . .
To think that I could leave myself on pages
And not be crumpled up
And thrown away . . .

I will go away
But not with him
And I leave not because I didn't love you
But . . . because I did . . .
Because I did

If there is a competition here of sadness
or rightness
or who has been the most understood
I concede . . .
Because I find it hard to explain my life any longer
I'm tired . . .
And perhaps . . . I have always been wrong

So . . . with only compassion for both of us
Some charity
No more faith . . . or hope
I give up to my weakness
I let it take me
It will not forgive me
And . . . neither will you

Think only of yourself now
Of the injustice
because
I am a stranger again
A prisoner of freedom
A hitchhiker . . .

I'll pray for you
. . . for us

And with useless love
I will say unwillingly
Finally
Good-bye

A LOUSY STORY

One last time
. . . You made me look at those wounds
The world knows . . . Don't worry
You have been the blessed saint
. . . I have been the sinner . . . You said it was
"A lousy story"

We forced each other to compromise until
Each of us had a certain control
. . . And it won't surprise anyone to know
That both of us resented the other
For allowing the other to do it . . .
Yes, we manipulated each other
How? . . . is too easy a question
We both carry a certain embarrassment about
How easily we did it . . .
The real question is
"Why" . . . And

Yes, I did leave you
On purpose . . . willfully
I was the adolescent leaving home
Knowing all the time
That I would be sorry later . . .
But I never pretended
It didn't matter . . .
I never tried to wash you off with Yardley soap
Or overlook your feelings

As a temporary stain . . . I did not regard you
As a used blade . . .
     . . . a dull miracle? . . . And
I never said it was
"a lousy story."

"We could make some use of this," you said
     . . . Not let this anger turn in against itself . . .
"Think well of me" . . . you said
And I do . . . when I can
I think well of myself as well
Of you and me together . . .
"Real understanding has majesty," you told me
And that's where the real victories are . . . So
If you must . . . Throw me up
Sweat me out
Enter other women to beat me down . . . But
I was not junk food . . . And this is not
"a lousy story."

ADAPTATION

It started in a simple room . . .
I made spitballs
Out of chocolate wrappers
And threw them from the balcony . . .
I hit my Grandmother on the chin . . .
And never forgave myself that cowardly assault . . .
. . . I think I know . . .
The ink on my Mother's bedspread
Yes—earlier that day
My first lie . . .
. . . That's where it all began . . .

And guilt still comes on
like a raging preacher . . .
My words hit your smile from New York
And slam into Grandmother's chin again . . .
This pain is further adaptation
(I can never forgive myself for a cowardly assault . . .)

And your leaving
Just brings you back
as hers did . . .
And both of you forgave me so easily
For all the names I call myself
I still remain
your Mary . . .

It started in a simple room
. . . and it continues . . .

NIGHT CRAWLERS

I'm sure what they say is true
. . . That we leave in pieces
That most robberies
occur at night
. . . That all murderers
Were lovers
First . . .

I'm a fugitive now
. . . Among those who keep passports
in their pockets
. . . I keep my car keys
As the outlaw kept his gun
Right beside
. . . the bed

So I'm sure what they say is true
. . . That we leave in pieces
Fearing not that we might miss each other
And scared to death
That
We may not . . .

LIFE INSURANCE

I've always left before the end
. . . Retired a champ
I left them all
Before . . .
They left me . . .

I always called the leaving freedom
But always it was safety
That I sought
. . . Leaving was insurance
Against
Being left . . . So

That's the truth
. . . That's the way it really was
Most every action I've ever taken
Has been
A reaction . . .

And yes it was men
Who cured me of men
. . . It was love
That healed me of love

And it may have been a coward's way
To leave a face before it turned on me
. . . To leave and be lost
Not sent away or
. . . Left . . . So

I always left before the end
. . . And it hurt us all a lot . . .
But lesser sure than staying on
Far less painful
Than having nothing left to leave . . .

So there it is . . .
If you need to know
. . . I loved them and I left them
But mostly . . .
I loved them . . .

THE COLLABORATORS

A good writer . . . She called you
And you are . . . and more
You hold controlling stock
On these pages
. . . I write about you
And for all your whining
About my not working with you
. . . This is collaboration
After all. . . .

"I love you . . . I'll take care of you . . . Trust
                                    me" you said . . .
"I'll carry your young
They will see the Nutcracker
We will be old in future landscapes"
Only trust is an offering . . . "Love is an
                                    investment for me"
But . . . you are already old. . . .

And you say that this is too brutal to be true
That you love me. . . . And I think you do love me
As much as you are capable of loving anyone
And only because you fear something in joy
Is joy not enough . . .

And yes . . . there is a lot of splendid in me
I am moving toward the more sacred . . . It's true
I have told you everything I know
Except this . . .

I'm a good writer, too
And for all this competition
. . . . You have written a book of me
I have come down another page of you
And we are
Collaborators
After all

FAULT LINE

Change is nobody's fault . . .
It comes faster though . . . I think
When we take aim
Or run toward something in the distance . . .
But even when it feels abrupt
When we finally hit the brakes and change direction
. . . Even then some thought precedes the move
No less than slower deaths
That come more silently
But get there just the same . . .
And . . .

It's nobody's fault
. . . that things can't stay the same
To freeze life in perfect patterns
is the antithesis of life
. . . death is the only metaphor
And the only other constant word that has

                                            no final defense
And it is nobody's fault
It comes faster though . . . I think
When we take aim
Run toward something in the distance . . .
And even when it comes abruptly
When we hit the brakes and push it to the floor
. . . Even then some thought precedes the move
No less than slower change
That comes more silently
But gets there just the same . . .
It's nobody's fault . . .

GAME PRESERVES

I cannot be reached . . .
Not by phone
Or finger
. . . My life is suspended
Not available
For now . . .
. . . I cannot be reached . . .

There is no movie sale in my holding out
. . . No mercy in my absentee ballot
No justice or permission
For this sudden strike
. . . There is no negotiation
From this vacancy . . .
No research
In these files . . .
I cannot be reached . . .

I no longer inhabit my face
. . . It continues without contact
The life muscle
Remembers
. . . habit and matter
Remain on duty
. . . The nerves accumulate
On battery . . .
The body guards its valuables
. . . The investment is secure
The land remains
. . . But

The executives offices are closed
. . . Decision is a open hole
And I would help you if I could . . . But
I'm not in uniform
And my spirit in escrow
Has no effect
. . . No legislation
In this present tense . . .

I cannot be reached
. . . There is no road
or reason . . .
There's been a holiday declared . . .
A week of Sundays
. . . a moratorium on feeling
The mind has overruled the cells
. . . And for now
You can touch me all you want . . .
You can get sick in my candy stores
You can reverse the charges
. . . But my life is unauthorized for now
My patent is pending . . .

I am immune to these proceedings
. . . I am a fugitive
By choice . . .
The truth is a blank form
. . . My flesh is winter clothing
My eyes are toy guards
. . . Feeling is a lost child
Holding its breath
. . . As long as it can

So . . . You can come over . . . if you like
You can window-shop
. . . Wait around until the doors open
Have a cup of coffee
. . . And you're welcome to use me
While I'm gone . . .
Start my motor
. . . Turn the soil . . . But

I cannot be reached . . .
Not by warrant
Or force . . .
My life is suspended
. . . My soul is unavailable to logic
The air has custody
. . . And you can touch me all you want
You won't leave a mark
Or memory . . .
Your fingerprints will not stay
On my breath . . . Because

The vacuum resides
. . . There are no names on the title
So . . .

Go ahead . . .
. . . I can see you're the kind
That will challenge these city halls
. . . You will fight my heart's bureaucracy
And lose . . . And

I'm telling you in this foreign tongue
That you're lost in this translation
. . . Your cock is useless
And your words are impotent . . .
. . . There are no entrances

You can leave a message
. . . Deposit your money
But . . . There is no interest
I will accept your application
And your hands . . .
. . . You can touch me all you want/But—
I cannot be reached . . .

WAITING FOR GODOT

In the photographs I have Panda eyes
. . . And you are the Hemingway face
(I always loved you in that raincoat)
Who would have guessed
That I was
the stronger?

Me . . . With all that puppyflesh
skinny yearling legs
And you read me passages from Balzac
And Beckett
. . . If not for you
I might still
Be waiting for Godot . . .

I'll say it is enough for any girl
To have her lover love her
To have the sight of someone seeing her
. . . Because of you
I am comfortable
with pleasure

In loving you
I learned to love men . . .
. . . It was your voice
That released me from any fear
That men couldn't cry out loud
Or keep
Their boyskin . . .

It was you who gave me absolution
. . . It was with your body
That I found the way to theirs

You . . . You who bought me the car
That I left you with . . .
You who gave me the gun that killed us
. . . You
Who couldn't have loved me more
If you loved me all your life
The man with the Hemingway faces
Who turned the devil's words
To music . . .

If not for you
. . . I might have seen pain as weakness
I might have overlooked the dignity of animals
. . . I might still
Be waiting for Godot . . .

I know I told you that I would love you forever
. . . But I really thought I would.
Who could have guessed that lifetime plans
Could be used up in five years
. . . Where I come from
People didn't leave each other
Just 'cause they left . . . And

I really thought I would stay all my life
. . . Even though I never have
Or could . . . But
I didn't lie . . . And

The girl who accepted
Your diamonds
Was not a jewel thief . . . So

Don't tell me that I loved you
So that I could write about it . . .
I wrote
. . . because I loved you

WHERE ARE THEY NOW?

Well—they say that he's been seen
with several girls
who look like her—
(he's very good
at adaptation)—

She lived alone in their house
like a bad child in her room
before she moved
to the beach
—the migratory Bird—

They have made some sense of these times
—if one is found in the other's arms
it is always as a guest
—they gave up their citizenship
Voluntarily—
his flesh is no longer
natural soil—

But at certain angles—
she can see his face before the accident
and
the past
is
fugitive again—

It's 5 A.M.—
My typewriter on empty
tired to the socks—

damn the body
it can bring every inspiration
to its knees
for a while—

But . . .
I want you to know this

As long as I'm awake
You'll always be alive

THE GIRL WHO KISSES FROGS

#1

I thought about this morning
The Humpty Dumpty girl
Who wanted to wear her head in your lap
On the grass
The easy Saturday morning songs
Picking for the clover
Foolin' around
Bein' goofy . . .

Hell . . . I know my innocence doesn't show
I'm a lighting expert . . . But
I haven't felt that way in years
Free falling
. . . Butterflies
Stage fright
That old enemy
The principal's office
Remember?

I could tell you it was something more
. . .
But I won't lie to you to get redemption
. . . You can't give it
I don't need it
I was just . . . Uncomfortable . . . That's all
I got the willies,
Remember?

Who knows why
Those bumps form on the skin
After all . . . It was only you
My green-eyed pleasure junkie
Easy like Bach
An early morning lotion
My friend
With the funny nose

But it's December
Isn't there always this Christmas rush
. . . Body to body
Dream to dream
Our work muscles
. . . Our thighs
Your open mouths coming into my smiles
. . . No, I can't let a lifetime pal like you
Be lost
For some Yankee lament
. . . I'll be there tomorrow
Cause these are the good old days
And
. . . It's almost Christmas

#2

So now you know
. . . As much as I don't like to admit it
I am the girl who kisses frogs
And sometimes your eyes do

Leave me unguarded
A direct line
. . . Your camera
And it gives me a rush
'Cause I really do want you to love me
Yeah I do
More than anything/almost
And besides
. . . It's almost Christmas

So . . . I don't care who sees us
We're not a student film
I love it when you drive us into the world in
                                    your brown bullet
When we spill ourselves on public streets
And that smile . . . That private smile
'Later Malloy . . . I will have you later'
And the hungry elevator kisses
The stolen bases in life
The simple hand holdings
I know I can't . . . But if I could
I'd take you home
. . . They woulda loved you

Nah . . . It can't be a sin to touch you
It can't be wrong to feel that good
. . . And if I've written songs for other men
You must know
You're not one of them . . .
I'm not saying you're the love of my life
The poet's jackpot

Even though you are
I guess all I'm trying to say is
That I really need you
Yeah . . . I do . . . A lot . . . And
. . . It's almost Christmas . . . So

You're a marksman
It's a bullseye
You can touch me anywhere
You're the only man who can
Or has
And the only guarantee is that I'm real
Not always right . . .

I always hoped I'd have that chance
To just be . . . With someone
To get the hiccups . . . You know
The hiccups . . .

So there it is . . . You know it all
Almost. . . . Or will . . . If you want to
So . . .

♯3

Could you be there in the morning
. . . Oh could ya?
'Cause it'd sure be good to see you
And it is
Almost Christmas?

You made breakfast for me
The awkward love
. . . child on Mother's Day morning—
Scraping the burn off the toast
You still don't know
That I will love you anyway . . .

If I never saw you again
. . . I would see you forever
We will never make the final payments
. . . For you and me
Everything
Is not enough . . . So

You can be the bashful boy this morning
. . . The carrier of life
Loving is not just women's work . . .

I will be your favorite ice cream
. . . You can take me slowly
Licking me
Reverently
Until . . .
I am all gone
(The boy in you is repaired)

You better watch out
You better not cry
Denver wins
So does Dallas
I'm not surprised
Roger Starbuck is a good Christian boy
And every dime-store cowboy in Denver
Deserves one good story to tell his grandchildren . . .
Jesus lives in Aspen
Commutes to Colorado Springs
Everybody knows . . .

And the bands play
Those airport songs
Again
While I crawl into my safety net
My brass home
Auld Lang Syne
My bed . . .

And I'm the perfect answer
For a man no longer asking questions
At least today . . .
'Cause my cousin went to Notre Dame
And I am the fighting elf
That laughs like a child
And makes love like
A woman . . .

New Year 78

Oh if only you could be here . . .
'Cause I made this quilt all by myself
For rainy days like this
Hot buttered love
The rare meat between my thighs
And hey . . .
You're no vegetarian . . .

Illegal procedure
Jungle moves
Pillow fights
The sandman lickings
The sheet suckers
Whisker burns . . . yeah
Whisker burns

My nipples like young soldiers—eager
Standing at attention—
Our mouths . . . like delinquents—defying every rule
Your mouth
Eating me
. . . alive

My milk
Comes to the doorway
To meet your mouth
And you rise
Like bread
Your eyes

Those headlights
Shut down

Want on want
Soul hunger
While I lick away
All your public faces
And I hear you moan
In your body's language
Suck me
. . . suck me
The soul
Begging for attention

And love
Rushes to my mouth
My heart
Is on its knees
And my syrup comes
That white blood
Down between my legs
My beauty spot

And I taste your salt
Your belly becomes my resting place
My Braille path
—aah—aah—
That lullaby
Intermission

Until your mouth
That sucking machine
Bites the Maryskin
Un do me . . . please
Untie the ropes
Set the children free
Open my gates
All of my life in your mouth
All of yours in mine
Who are the fools who think
That mother's milk
Is dry?

Your eyes open like
A heat lamp
And we stare at each other
Paralyzed
Together
A silent life scream
While our bodies
slide in
And out of each other's souls

You take aim
The cream rises
The volume full blast
You don't scream
But
You scream

Your bullets hit
my bullseye
You've touched me
With more than your body
And
I cry . . .

And that is life . . . I think
That offering
Our morning prayers said
The cherished
Afterlaughs
The melancholy
The private concerts
The Sunday times

I don't want to say something
Like I love you
That's not enough . . . it never is
But it takes too long to translate
Any other way. . . .
It's New Year's Day . . .
And I want you to know
If there was a God
I'd pray for us . . . pray that he keep us
Safe . . . and free
But mostly free . . .

You're an honest pleasure McGee
An honest pain

A Yankee punk
I'd send you flowers . . . if I could
And more than that . . .
You know I would

This is the Harvest year
Enjoy!

INFLATION

You have brought them back to me
. . . You are the young Robert
In my teen-age arms
You are the Nana who had a wishing tree
. . . You are the children's Charlie
The good giant . . . So

It's no matter that we pay a dime
For penny candy
. . . Because you kissed me
And all the strangers left my mouth
. . . You are with me in Paris
Where Revoux played the mandolin
. . . You whistle
And he's home again . . .

You have brought them back to me
. . . All the boys who turned to men
Everyone who loved me then . . .
. . . It's no matter that we pay a dime
For penny candy
. . . no matter
At all . . .

PANIC AT THE
ALIBI LOUNGE

These things are not supposed to last
. . . You can't have me with your morning coffee
Aren't you the man who told me
You could never spend the night?

These things are not supposed to work
. . . lead to times like these
The whole idea is to 'want each other'
Not 'have each other'
I think we've missed the point . . .

You see . . .
These things are not supposed to be wonderful
They're supposed to hurt like hell
. . . We're supposed to drink white wine in obscure cafés
Make love in the afternoon and go home
. . . But not together!!!
This is all wrong . . .

Sure . . . A stolen weekend is classic
Making love five times before noon
But we've been together for a year . . .
I think we've forgotten the rules
. . . These things are simply not designed to last . . .

The concept is to want it . . .
Not to have it . . .
We're supposed to be seduced and deprived

Not touched and blessed . . .
I'm telling you
. . . We're not very good at having an affair . . . See

I'm supposed to be crying all the time
. . . You should be paying cash instead of credit cards
At some point . . . Months ago . . . We should have had
                                        a painful fight
You should be very moody . . . not such
                                        a celebrant . . . Hey
Your attitude is all wrong!!

I don't think we're supposed to be this happy
. . . I've read all the novels
For all the passion and glory of the lovers . . .
It was always the leaving
And not the coming
That made the stories work . . . Hey

They're not going to like this . . .
All our friends are going to look like fools
. . . For all their tales of our leaving each other
                                        and going home
We are home together . . . And
Even though things like this don't last for them
Things like this always last with us . . . So

We screwed it up . . . So what . . .
We'll have other chances . . .

REVISION

We made it!!!
No, you didn't kiss me
under the 'Bridge of Sighs'
But you did take me
To Venice . . .

No, I'm not pregnant
And we're not poor
But we do love each other a lot . . . And
This is New York . . .
We made it!!!

For all the times we fell a little short
The defeats were not final
. . . And don't you know
The love we make in Aspen
Is just as sweet as all the love we'll make
in St. Moritz
. . . For all my lunches in Paris
I'll take our cold white wine
in Santa Fe . . . Because

We are everywhere
. . . When we're together
For all the first class tickets
. . . It is your arms
That bring me to New York

. . . Your love
That makes the city
beautiful . . .

No, I'm not the first in your bed
Your body is not my only education
But . . . just as surely
This is love
That has never been made before . . . And

No, we don't have our play
On Broadway . . . That's true . . . But
We do have it here
On West 58th Street
And . . .

Anything is possible
. . . As long as waking up together
Is everywhere
We want to be . . . So

We made it!!!
For all the dreaming
We are the dream . . .
For all the travel plans
All the planes are useless
Unless they bring me to you . . .

And I am scared
Scared because it's scary . . .
Because You are the way You are
Because I am the way I am . . .
A rush of pure music
A lonely melancholy
Scared because things are not always as they seem
Because things are always the way they are . . .

The truth is . . . You can't leave without me anymore
And I can't be alone . . . Because you are in me now
And my greatest fear is not that your love may not last
But that my own will not survive
'Cause I'm a sprint runner,
And if I break your heart
It will hurt you for a long time
But it will hurt *me*
FOREVER . . .

I'm not saying that I'll be first in the locker room
To audit the lies . . .
Or that I want détente from your thoughts . . .
That promise
I only want to say that you leave a hole in my life
                                        when you're not here
And that you cannot leave without me anymore . . .

And I have had most of the things a girl could have
                                        in this life
Men enough to notarize the woman in me forever
Love enough to testify as my proudest legacy
Success enough to simplify my ambition . . .

So I want you to know this much
These are not coincidences
That I spend these hours at this typewriter
And not somewhere else
This is not a folly.

The only thing I'll always have is the ability
To actually BE where I am
And you can't leave without me . . . Anymore
We are not ships passing in the night
But the night allowing the ships to pass through us

It was change that brought me to you . . .
                                    It was my spirit caught
And that may be the same thing that robs me from you
But you can be sure . . . whatever else . . . That
                                    you can't leave
without me anymore . . . Even when I'm not here to leave
So I pray that I don't break your heart
It will hurt you for a long time
But it will hurt me . . . FOREVER

THE WAY THINGS ARE

You know . . .
I always thought I knew
About these things
That the simple sounds of the gulls
Returning to the pier at night
Would be music enough
And it is . . .
. . . sometimes . . .

But there's a sorrow tonight
. . . in me
No, not an unforgiving pain
Or a remembering of something lost
No . . . it's not that easy to explain . . .
It's more like the feeling a child gets
At a Bambi movie
"Why are you crying?" they would ask me
"Why? . . . I don't know why . . ."
Maybe because Bambi's mother dies
Or maybe because I so loved those animals
But it was always more than that . . .
It was . . . because
That's the way things are . . . damn it
That's the way things are . . .

And the simple ways things are
Sometimes leave an undefinable sorrow in me
A first time away from home lonesome

And it's in me . . .
In you . . . And damn it . . .
That's the way things are . . .

I just wanted you to know
That I know . . .
I know there are moments too private for literature
Or pages like these . . .
And I know that you're troubled . . .
That you pay a price
For your time with me . . .
And I want to rock it away
. . . Have the good guys win
But there are no bad guys in this story
No . . . not a single one.

I want too much . . .
I say too much
. . . It's probably true . . .
That I'm slightly mad
But you must never think
That I don't understand
Because . . . I always thought that the simple
                                    sound of the gulls

Returning to the pier at night
Would be music enough
But sometimes . . . it isn't . . . and
damn it . . .
That's the way things are . . .

And
We *are* dangerous
Because we ride the thermals in life
Because we are savage believers
And because we force the true
Out of our own experience
Because we long for miracles
When most people are afraid of them . . . But

I'll *never* be sorry—

I want to give you something important
Because your smiles are heirlooms now
And I'm not afraid to say
That you've changed my life
Applauded my small lights
Until they grew so proud
No one will ever
Blow them out . . .
And I want for you
The highest kind of gifts
A lifetime flight like mine
Over friendly beaches
And porches strewn with bread crumbs
Because of all the men I've known
No other had your vision
To see the boy's reflection in the puddle
To know that dogs have pals, too
And because you stop and consider
The rain's design on windshields

I know that you can cry
I know . . .

And we *are* dangerous—
'Cause when you're open wide as us
The nerves need explanation
We have an airport sad
Hit and run melancholy
Pa rum pa pum pum—

But . . .
The wings are not reluctant—I promise you
There are no guilty birds!!!

THE EARLY SONGS

I want to say something to you perfectly
And maybe not again . . .
Not because it may matter someday
But because
It matters now . . .

And the words are here unedited
Without publishers or copyright
Never to appear on any page
For sale . . . (well . . . almost never.)

You're beautiful
You really *are* gifted
Yes . . . Talented too
But that's not what I mean
You're exciting by your own excitement
Touched by your own touching . . . and

Layer by layer
White on white
The scared comes off of me
Forever

And
You've not been to Laural Valley

It wasn't you who sent me dandelions
Who wanted all babies to have my eyes
No . . .
You are *not* one of them

And here I am
Your sap dripping from me
Your sweet wet mouth
Held in trust
Upstairs

And my funny bones have
Held over from an eastern summer
When I had no motives
Only appetites

And there will be others
And there will be more
But . . . not like you
And . . . not like this

And you've domesticated your guilt
Forgiven yourself ambition
A Gatsby mellowed
Nailed to your life
Charming . . . Sturdy

Your vulnerability only makes you
The more splendid

And I'm a renegade clown
Sure . . . sleek as a racehorse . . . well-trained
They say I pray on airplanes
But you can't believe everything you hear

I've been Cinderella more than once
In spite of all my A's
My cold white wine
I was bred to jump fences
I can't be killed by ordinary bullets

And here we are
All of our proud spots showing
Immigrants from a philosophy class
A watercolor Matisse

Tourists in each other's lives
Walking high wires
Making love
That will never be recorded
In anyone's biography

And what a gift you are
. . . Uncomplicated
No scorecards
A common charity

Love is . . . I think
An unconditional generosity

I don't know if I've said it all
. . . Or perfectly
But I just wanted you to know . . . today
All day
That I do . . .
. . . Love you I mean
Even if it's with stumbling tongue
And clumsy words like these

And . . . we are not location thunder
No . . . Don't tell me that
I never drink on New Year's Eve
Besides . . .
I'm busy

So . . . let's crowd you into these few days
All your indoor faces
I'll sleep with you at every age
And lick you clean of everything but me
And we'll learn to laugh in every language
And be all the things we dreamed about when we were ten

So go make your movies . . .
I'll write your songs
In every way that matters
You're covered
You're the closest Tracy I've ever found
To my Hepburn . . .

I've been to the south of France
When the sun was on fire
And I have travel posters in my mind
That no agent ever saw . . .
But nothing's ever moved me quite the same
As seeing you
In certain light . . .

So . . . All I want to say
I guess . . . is
You're the best vacation
I've ever had . . .

So don't go around thinking
That I won't miss you
. . . 'cause I will
And I know I shouldn't say this
But . . . what the hell . . .
Any hands but yours
Would be a sacrilege to me . . .
And no amount of wine or sun
Can make that go away . . .
There is no other man that cuts this deep
No room to let him try . . . 'cause
That's a gift you can't give twice
No matter how you lie . . .

So even though I never expected to
. . . I love a Yankee punk . . .
I mean—I always knew it would take more
than a few Hail Mary's

To set me free . . .
Exempt from mortal sin . . .

I know this . . .
People don't end
Because pictures do . . . But
What I didn't know
Is that a girl like me
Can't love a man like you
For a while . . .
And that every rule and map I have
Is useless way up here
There were no signs . . . on any roads
That could have told me
I could love
Without a motive in my mind . . . except
To simply love . . .
When all the generosity in me is released
When every good thing I know about myself
Is finally . . . true
So . . . In different ways
For different reasons
Some of us get away without drugs
Or God . . . or promises . . . but
I've done all that

I've had all the faith
and Moroccan hash a girl could want . . .
I've been to the south of France
I have travel posters in my mind
That no travel agent ever saw . . .

But nothing's ever moved me quite the same
As seeing you
. . . in certain light . . . So
Don't go around thinking
That I won't miss you
. . . 'Cause I will . . .

IN HONOR OF YOU

In honor of you
I'll hug my children that much longer
And there will be
Lamb chop bones and liver
For "Old Faithful"
Everyone will celebrate what you have done to me . . .

And he'll be there tomorrow
Hungry and vulnerable
Begging to be safe
And I'll fatten him with smiles
Sing him every song he wants to hear
Because of you
I'll be the girl he prayed for

I feel
Released
There is more of me
More of you
More of everything to share
With more of them

And we did not take one thing
From one another
Imagine that . . . civilized pleasure

Unconditional caring
Isn't a small monument

Better than before
We are

Even with this leaving

And in your honor
In mine
I'll share you on my tables
I'll stretch myself . . .
I'll stay a little longer

STAYING ALIVE

Our love is not mature
or housebroken
—it is still a social hazard
I know I will lie to protect it—

        I want to stay alive

Anxious to be the one
I cannot forget
Your eyes are open
when you touch me—
Your passion
grows knots
I fear
the holes
you will leave—

You want to stay alive—

On purpose
I forgot to tell you that
he will never hurt you—
He will not kill what I love
He will kill
what he loves and

        I want to stay alive

For a moment
we have seen the devils
in each other
—the stranger
—In those moments
religion became a possibility
For a moment—and by design
each thought the other
was insane
—Mirror images—our eye teeth bare—
Much more alike
than we are different

We want to stay alive

In a moment of utter truth
You know that you would cry for me
But you are not a tourist at funerals
You don't have the courage to keep me
Or . . .
To let me go—so
I'll dare you with this strange neglect
To become the man I'm afraid you are
. . . the final one

THE MALIBU JOURNALS

What fine days these are . . .
. . . A strong surf
Lemon sun
. . . And the butterscotch of late afternoon
Overture of amber light
. . . Egg yolks and strawberries on the horizon at seven
A skyfire!

And the beach dogs
The hounds . . .
. . . Fifteen of them, at least
A convention
Of hearts
. . . The fuzzy loyals
Of the world . . .

And . . .
You are by the ocean, too
. . . Just north an hour
On Cole Porter's ranch
. . . The last stronghold
Sand all stuck
To your dreams
. . . What fine days
These are . . .

And by the time the new Ivy
has climbed the lattice

and reaches the deck
. . . I will have loved you
Another winter

. . .

   . . .

     . . .

And Molly
. . .

Her Father doesn't know it
But I think fondly of him
Now and then . . .
After all . . . He did make her a cradle
With his hands
. . . The young Lincoln

I never told him
. . . But I thought I heard him crying
The night we left
. . . And it broke me
That sound
. . . That late sorrow

Anyway . . . It's been a long time
Dark spots
. . . I want to parole the past
Let it yield
. . . Untethered
Like the early songs

. . . his law books
The chords of his piano
. . . the Molly love
When we all shared the same
dog . . .
. . .
. . .
. . .

It's a privilege . . . I think
To live on the floor of the sand
. . . To sleep at the entrance to the sea
Lime green November breezes
. . . Wintergreen
And

The holidays are here
Certified with cranberries
. . . A family heart
Underscored by punt returns
Pumpkin pies . . .
. . . Sure . . . it's corny
But what can you expect
. . . This isn't literature
And . . .
The holidays are here

. . . Who could be more sentimental
Than me . . . In my bikini
On the deck
. . . The romantic hypocrite

My white meat basted
Under the brown
. . . A holiday Turkey

And Suzanne drives from Santa Cruz
. . . A lift ticket pinned to her only jacket
All her revolutions have turned to
whole wheat symphonies
. . . The simple cotton weave of her clothes
as we stuff the bird like Mother did
. . . Passing the baton on to Molly and to Mac . . .
Wondering if we'll ever taste pretzels
from a tin can again—

MARY'S LAMB

Take me . . . I said
Bring me to my knees
Before I'm too strong to be taken
Murder my careers
Cure my sophistication
Break my beauty hard
Against the kitchen floor and
Take me . . .
Bring me to my knees . . .

On the street
We are fair game
To the untrained eye
And it's too late and too soon
To die strangers
Anymore

'Cause I'm the one you prayed for
From your rookie bunk
The one you feared
Would come . . .

And I want you more than I dare admit . . .
I want you from my childhood
I want you from my toes
I want you from the beginning
And if you left
It would take a hundred men
To fill the holes . . . Because

I want you with my body's mouth
You make my heart come
. . . that funny bone . . .

And if we live
I'll follow your car through traffic
Like a duckling running faster and faster
As if losing sight of you
Would freeze me lost forever

And I do want you to be my Daddy
Give me absolution
As you lift my dress
And aim your love
'Cause you have that patch of hair
                                        just above the knuckle . . .
And I'm counting on you
To stay alive . . .

'Cause you're a streetfucker
The one I dreamed about
The barroom jock
Who healed my reality . . .

So . . . If I hide
It's mostly from myself
'Cause in me resides
That animal you saw and wanted
Who saw you . . .
That female
Who cries as though her skin were raw

But when she cried
She always cried
For more . . .

And I am all the girls
You've always dreamed about
. . . And none of them
I am the one with the birthmark
Whose eyes lock your life
As you stare crazy from my thighs
I know what you are thinking
. . . I even know why . . .

You're a streetfucker
A temporary genius
A purebred
On the front lines
A primal need
Classic pain
Oh no, we won't be subtle . . .

I'll say it now
Because it's finally true
We are not crazy
And this time together
Is as close to doing what we were born to do
As any film . . . Or book . . . Or child
                              we leave behind . . .

If there's a God . . .
He's turned our blood to wine

And my thighs have seen the glory
And he prays from the eyes
To be seen . . . as that passion
My body is a church that you enter worshipping yourself
And we may be annihilated/we may die

                               until a real death is ordinary
But we will be God's symphony/awesome/breathtaking
A freefall . . . A Marymount fantasy—But . . .
I will always be God's toy . . . turned real
And you will be Mary's lamb . . .

YOU WEREN'T THE ONLY ONE

Listen . . .
I stuck my tongue out at the sisters
I've blamed the economy
On the Republicans . . .
I've believed what I've read
In the papers . . . So

Airplanes can be made
Out of paper . . .
Their arms can reach out
Across the ceiling of the sky . . .
And we can come to this
From children in the city
Who walk barefoot on hot asphalt
. . . You weren't the only one
Who saw the heat design
The patterns in the air . . .
You weren't the only one who
Examined the eyes of animals
For an understanding
Hey . . . I've checked dollar bills for flaws . . .

Listen . . . Questions start in the muscle
Just as they did
With the citizens of Rome
. . . You're not the only one
Who reads the funnies first . . .
And whether you take your hands away

. . . or not
I will love them just the same//
I will eat meat on Fridays . . .
I will kiss frogs . . .

So . . . name me first . . .
And make me the oldest . . . But
You still won't be the only one
Who eats the middle out of the cookie
first . . .

MORE OF LESS

You want immortality . . . You say . . .
To sacrifice these days with friends
To be remembered later by strangers?
. . . A legacy on film and found in libraries . . .
You want to live forever . . .
Good insurance for the soul with little faith . . .
You want to live forever
. . . *I want to live now* . . .

And I would rather my children remembered
That I loved you
That I touched them
. . . Oh, I would rather that
Than—
They remember me as writer
I would rather that
They remembered their childhood/starved by this Mother
. . . Who could sacrifice these days with them
. . . To be remembered later by strangers . . .

You want immortality . . .
To stay beyond the leaving
. . . To multiply life
You want to be remembered by people not yet born
. . . even at the expense of being forgotten
By those of us already here . . .
And that is what I've tried to say all night . . .
. . . the difference has always been the same

94

. . . You want me to love you forever and
I want you to love me now . . .

And as for immortality?
It doesn't come for those of us who exchange
                                    the present tense
for future applause . . .
Immortality . . . if it comes at all
is *always* a belated gift . . .
However long it lasts . . . however large . . .
It always comes too late . . .
Too late . . .

JANUARY 10, 1978

He bought me a ring today
It was plastic . . .
But . . . It wasn't an imitation
Or a perfect replica . . .
It was just as real as playing doctor
. . . Just as real

We are the blind children
Who live on the edge of the cliff
And we have no plans
No silverware
No pedigree
Or seal of approval

We live in a southernmost heart
On a fault line
We come hard
And evaporate within the hour
We bleed
Invisible ink . . .

We eat love that we grow ourselves
And we speak a language
That has no translation
We perform our own abortions

We are among the people
Who die together

But . . . Who never live together
We are bound by plastic rings
The color of children's cheeks
And

We are just as real
As the dolls in your baby carriage
When you still believed that big people
Knew everything
We are just as real as the Boogie Man
. . . Just as real

Ambition
Can be a terrible poverty
. . . Inherently, it means
That we are always less
Than we want to be
. . . That the primal peace eludes us

As long as we are ambitious
. . . There is always more . . . And ironically
There is never
Enough . . .

THE IROQUOIS

Last night you let me talk and talk
Not for what I said
. . . But just to say it . . .
As I did those final nights at summer camp
Just not to fall asleep
Not let those final mornings come so easily . . .

On the first Sunday in September every year
They came to take us . . .
And we'd never pack our trunks until we heard them
on the bridge
My brother's whistle through his teeth
. . . The signal hope was gone
And my bunk was just another bunk again . . .

And every year I'd promise
To write and call
Keep the secret code
And wear my shark's tooth necklace
Out into the world
A sure sign I was among the "Fearless Eight"
They call "The Iroquois"

And the station wagons pulled away
. . . the turnpike lines the passage to another home
From ten long weeks
The slow dissolve began . . .

And all the clichés are important
George M. Cohan still makes me cry
It's no secret
That I still have a hard time
Betting against Notre Dame
No matter what the spread . . .

So . . . It doesn't surprise me at all
That I cry in airports
That a boarding call could signal still that
Hope is gone . . . And that my mouth in leaving yours
Was just another mouth again . . .

The planes pull away
The runway lights the passage to another home
It doesn't surprise me at all to know
That I have a hard time throwing away old sneakers
Because no matter what . . . I'll write and call
I'll never break the secret code
I'll be back . . . you'll see . . . Because I still have
                    my shark's tooth necklace—And . . .
I'll always be among the "Fearless Eight"
They call
"The Iroquois"

OUTLAWS

The plane leaves in an hour
And when it touches down . . .
. . . We will be married again
But not to each other . . .

I'm afraid I'll say too much
And . . . not enough

Straining at the seams
Both to keep you
And . . . To let you go

To catch a shirt tail
A piece of trouser

The words come slower now
Because they are more
Important

This typewriter
. . . My grand piano
I don't want to play it
Anymore . . .

So . . . I just want to say
This last thing
That it's really good to know
That two people

Can touch each other
Without leaving scars or dents

It's good to know
That even outlaws
Like you and me
Can ride the world unnoticed
And still have
Our membership
Home . . .

Our plane leaves in an hour
And tonight we'll be home
Making love in our own bed
But
Not to each other . . .

MAGEE'S MAGIC BOX

This is a magic book . . .
For poets and word painters
Crazy Irish playwrights
And fools . . .

It doesn't have to be important in the world of ideas . . .
It's a place to keep the photographs you take
                                    without cameras
It's for keeping beautiful strangers
And foreigners . . .
Fantasies
And fables . . .

It's for prayers
And primitive pleasures
And gifts you give yourself . . .
It's a book where you can write symphonies
And make love . . .

It's a good place to put used feelings
To remember or forget . . .
It's a place to release imaginary balloons
Get mad
Or fat
Be dumb
Get strong . . .

It's for the pursuit of innocence
It's for describing in Braille
A shorthand biography
It's a safe place to describe those miracles
That no one ever sees but you . . .
It's a place where you can nurture young ideas
Brave new films
Tax-free interest
In yourself

Yep . . . It's a magic book . . .
Made by elves
Like mine
Especially for fools . . .
Irish playwrights
Word painters
And poets . . .
Like you . . .

And . . . after it's written
You'll never be lost
. . . to anyone that ever knew you
Or . . . Wanted to . . .

So there!

ERNIE'S ALMANAC

And . . .
No matter what Ernie says
I'm not in love with you
I'm not . . .
Don't smoke or drink either
And . . . I'm tall
5'6" at least
The altitude alone keeps me high
It isn't easy
Being an Amazon

So . . . I'm not in love with you
I'm not . . .
I think you're sweet
Even though you're not
Entirely . . . And like I said . . . you are a beauty
Not a conventional one . . .
I mean . . . a mug like yours
Does not come down the pike
Every day

And I always could
Make more love
Than money
So
Don't go around thinkin'
I'm stuck on you . . . or something

I always act like an idiot
And hang around
Downtown Hollywood

You know my philosophy
Life just isn't worth dying for
It just isn't
The cover of *Time*
A chance at the Rose Bowl
Those are the really important things
In life.

So
Just in case
You've been kidding yourself
I ain't no editing room groupie—see
I'm a no-nonsense producer
My mind weak
From too much responsibility
And work
I want you to know
I let everybody grab my ass
In the hallway
That's right . . . old ladies . . .
Pre-school boys
I don't care . . . I'm easy

And thousands of directors
Have traveled up my thighs
For years—
Hell . . . I ain't got no pride

So don't go around thinkin' you're special
'Cause I'm tall
And tall people are mean
But love you? . . .
You're a punk
You who gave me VD
On my lip
You should know—
I never sleep in my own room
When I'm out of town
It's against my religion—and no matter what Ernie says
Producers just don't fall in love
With directors
It's against Guild rules

Here we are hanging by the pages
Connected by the threads of some old courage
Expecting mercy in exchange
For all the years we sat behaved . . .
Knowing this might come.

Surely lying can't be worse than this . . .
This honesty is brutal
. . . More confining a freedom than I imagined
I want you to go home
. . . While there's still time . . .
I want you to go home. . . .

And if by chance . . .
We're saved from this . . .
If this brave young script comes through
Galloping like a mindless soldier
Carrying our flags onto center stage . . .
Would that be more a celebration
. . . Or last rite . . . ?
I'm afraid to look . . . aren't you?
Afraid that mercy comes with justice if at all . . .
And to think that we could hang here . . .
Not making a move in fear that we might fall
Connected by a fear of death
That turned to fear of life . . .
Hanging by the pages of a script

Knowing that our lives are determined by committees
Here we are . . . expecting mercy in exchange

For all the years we sat behaved
. . . Knowing this would come . . .

If both our lives have come to this . . .
If all the love we have combined cannot heal the truth
Then surely lying can't be worse than this . . .
And all the years we sat behaved
All the years we sat behaved . . .

Was it you I saw in the woods?
. . . I was only eight years old that September
. . . a third grade soldier at St. Pius
I didn't know that men like you remembered
little girls like me . . .

"I saw a sailor in the woods today"
My voice less credible beneath the dinner conversations
. . . smaller too . . . because I often made things up
                                          like that . . .
The older ones had memories and larger sentences . . .
. . . I wondered if I could ever spell the words
                              they said . . . or understand
. . . "On a ship, Mary?" My brother laughed . . .
"Did the sailor come to port down by the creek?"
And I had no defense at all . . . guilty as I was so often then
Of telling tales . . . guilty now of making up the truth
. . . "Oh no, I really did . . ." I whined . . .
                           "He was six feet tall and looked
A lot like Uncle Pete . . . C'mon . . . I really did"
"This time . . . I really did" . . .

And now you're here . . . And
I didn't know till now . . .
That we remembered in proportion to our size
You were taller then . . .
Much taller then . . .

"I want to spend my life with you" It was hard for me
                                 to say out loud . . .
My voice increased because the words are finally true . . .

After all the times I've said them . . . all the men I've tried
to fit to the words . . . I say . . . "I love You" . . .
"Sure you do" . . . The wisdom in you misdirected . . .
"You love me like you loved all the others you were going
to spend your life with??"
And again I had no defense at all . . . and I knew that you
were going to make the truth a lie . . . With the cruelest
logic you assume . . .
and here I am . . . the teller of the tales . . . beating away
the Karma justice . . . Screaming now for my third grade
sailor . . . From all my hearts . . . Even though it is no
use . . . And never was . . . Still . . . I cry . . .
"Oh no, this time I really do" . . . Damn it . . .
"This time, I really do"

THE WINTER GAMES

I'm allowed to see you
With a visitor's pass
To take you off the lot for lunch
If you're back by two . . .
I can call you while the switchboard's open
And if I can't reach you by six
. . . I can't reach you . . .
On the weekends you're home
But . . . You don't live with me
The gates of your home
Have no visitors like me
And the public phones
Are much safer
Than your private lines . . .

Angry
. . . Sure I'm angry
Like you
. . . I'm a visitor

CREDITS

It is the fear of all composers
That they might underscore
The singers on piano
And be called accompaniment . . .
Is it such a malicious thought
To rest a bar—tap your foot
And be called simply a musician?

Is it the fear of all choreographers
That they might dance their own designs
And be regarded as third from the right?
Is it such a malicious thought
To be fabric in your own design and
Fear that they might think
You only dance?

It was hard for you today
To be so undefined
Not to be remembered as author and
Regarded as accompaniment . . .
But isn't it the fear of all designers
That their fabric be called clothes?
Isn't it the fear of all architects
That their houses become homes?

1538 39TH ST.

There are two images
Leapfrogging

He remembers being alone
But he wasn't . . .

The trembling
. . . The anger
Came later

The photographs come
In layers . . .
Peeling
. . . Changing

Only the address
Stays the same . . .

He remembers being alone
But he wasn't.

No matter what they say . . .
. . . We always live in that first house
We will always remember
Catholics on Fridays

How could he have known then
That everything would change
. . . Except
The address . . .

PUBLIC NOTICES

The fever has broken . . .
We no longer stand convicted of all the atrocities
Our names have been cleared . . . lipstick off
                                        the washroom walls
Our obscure passions released for publication
                                        to the trade . . .

Forgiven for being human
That final similarity

. . .
Not that I'm keeping score
Or planning a shoot-out
Hoping for overtime attempts to beat the spread
. . . I don't want to leave a scar
Or break the bank
Abuse tradition
Nah . . .

It's just that nowhere else on Earth
Can people be so proud of their humility
. . . The highest mix of metaphor prevails
A community that dreams awake
Tortured by their greatest pleasures
Bound in knots by freedom

VALENTINE

Bless Pete Ferguson and Gracie Schwartz
. . . Because they did it for us
They loved each other with our love
They carried our seeds
Used our tickets well
God bless Pete and Gracie

They took all the flights we missed
And . . . Because of them
We are more . . . And
We are always together

With their eyes
I saw you
With their feelings
I understood my own
With their hands
You touched me
And when they held each other
We were in their arms

They touched the people that we reached for . . .
And they signed our names
. . . Messengers they were
When they walked into the Emerald Bar
. . . We arrived

Oh, bless Ferguson and Schwartz
. . . Because they did it for us

They celebrated our lives with their own
And every word they said
We meant . . .
And when Pete gave the world the finger
He used our anger
Our wine turned to his blood
And because Gracie died our death
We will
Always be alive . . .

Bless them
. . . Because they were born from us
Born old
And grown young
. . . And because of them
We are more . . . And
We will always be together.

(I.E., STEINBECK)

We talk about fighting the world
Like a couple a teen-age runaways
. . . we build monuments in words
For the little guy on the page
Who bucks the system
And breaks his ass
To prove that cancer does not kill the mice
. . . it's been the lab technicians all along
. . . At last . . . The true cause of cancer
In mice . . .
And men . . . If you like
(. . . If they've got a minute George
Tell them again about the rabbits . . .
The rabbits . . .)

We listen to music as though the writer
wrote the songs especially for us . . .
As though he knew we would feel this way today
When he wrote it eighteen months ago . . .
Oh, they've got us . . . Those sweet songs
As long as there's a radio . . . they can shoot us
with sadness . . . slide us back together . . .
pull us apart again . . . Rip!
It hurts so good . . . and with each word
They get closer to the life nerve
Disguised as love songs
They've got us . . .

They get us in that part of us that sneaks away
                                    and grows up . . .
They get us in that part of us that never does . . .
They get us in our own children's nursery rhymes
They get us in the community of property of dreams
of log cabins and library cards . . .
They've got us . . .

They get us by the balls of our faithful dogs
By the fabric that we love on the sofa
By the way they know what to say and do
Before it's said and done . . .
They get us with a shorthand . . . Ham hocks
Pension plans and dues of every color and kind.
They get us in the daily mail
Through a front door . . . that locks from both sides
and is always opened . . .
Front doors are the last illusion
Because . . . They've got us . . .

They've got us by our lies
'Cause even when we're gone
They know . . .
We can still be reached by phone and wine . . .
They've got us by the bristles on our toothbrushes
The names on our checks
They've got us by memories
Photographs
Report cards and antiques . . .
They've got us . . .

They've got us like the Germans
Who couldn't leave what they couldn't take
What they couldn't carry . . .
They've got us by our cedar chests
By our joint returns
And common numbered cards . . .
They've got us by a money that doesn't grow on trees
. . . They got us by our past . . . Our history
By the shirttail of an earlier dream
By melancholy
By songs we used to love
And stories we used to tell
They've got us . . .

The freedom eaters work hard into the night
. . . And they get us by our darkest weakness . . .
They get us 'cause we want too much
'Cause we want to have it all . . .
Even them . . .
They got us 'cause we signed for the machinery
That engineered our own destruction
They got us straight through the heart
By our pain . . . Our guilt
Our beauty . . . Our pleasure
They got us by our burial plots
And later by insurance
Oh . . . They got us . . .
(They got us good . . .)

So for those of us who must drive blindly
At any speed . . . And we always will

. . . To stay alive . . . We must be on familiar land
Use familiar eyes . . . Not drive foreign cars
In our native soil . . .
Because they've got us nailed . . .
To crosses they've carried for us
The giving trapped us in a receiving line
. . . And we ignore the signs . . . the traffic reports . . .
The scales and the blood pressure . . .
We overdraw all the accounts . . .
While our fat souls occupy
Our bankrupt bodies
Checkmate hell
This ain't no game that anybody wins for long . . .

So you can tell me again about the rabbits
. . . Or I'll tell you . . . It doesn't matter
'Cause we are the same color in the dark anyhow
We salute the same flag
A small resistance movement . . . that could
                                        change the world
. . . Find a cure for chicken soup
Or a decent cause for this effect . . .

We are brilliant at believing . . .
We have nuclear imaginations
. . . muscles that pump love into our lives
Even when we're asleep

. . . We are a natural enemy
A natural energy
A homemade/hand-knit machine-made guarantee
We are a tradition . . . now

We've been in the family for years

We've earned the right to fight the world
To build monuments to madness
For the little guy who bucks the system
And breaks his ass to prove that nothing can be proven
                                        but the pudding
'Cause we've paid our taxes . . . our tolls . . . our tips
Our tuition and our ten percent
We drank our milk/ate our vegetables
Went to low cholesterol/high calonics
Rising signs and lowered tar and nicotine
We've been citizens of Cain
And Able
County, state, country, continent
Area code and zip
We've lost our parents, our minds
Our receipts
And our winnings . . .

And they've got us . . .
On the same laser line
Where we have them
Equal parts
The equal hearts amendment
They've got us by our titles . . . Registered and Sealed
In every writer's guild
And baptismal font
In every name we've used
Or been called
They've got us . . .

They've got us where it matters
In the confessional . . . On the mat
Kneeling at our own feet
So don't waste any more time making reservations
(Or having them)
You're confirmed as a prisoner of war
A soldier at a desk job
A foreign legion.

We've been linked to Van Gogh
And Gatsby
The very young/The very old
The very rich/The very poor
We've been seen by working aunts
Nurses' aides and
Spies who loved us . . .

We've been budgeted/boarded/cast and shot
We've been rated by Neilson/polled by Gallup
Tested on the toughest roads
By the meanest drivers
We've been a scandal/a sacrament/an exaggeration/
                               a disappointment/a surprise
We've been the first hope/the last hope/the only hope
We've been the scourge of our neighborhoods
And its triumph
We've been shocked/hurt/healed/hated and had
We've been up against Charlie's Angels
Double digit unemployment
And the wall . . .
We've been on television

And drugs . . . More than once
We've been polluted/inflated/mortgaged
And sold
We've been underlined/overruled/understated
                                          and overpriced
We've been everywhere but in the middle/on the news/
                                          on the nose

We've done everything but do it
We've said everything but say it
We'll be paying dividends for years
But
We've never been rewritten
Released or returned
No one's changed our numbers, our names
Or our minds
We're the last stronghold left
Front-line fools/poets
and Irish playwrights

Gentle Men with knives we'll never use
'Cause we got em good with magnum charm
And rosebuds in the bath
We are the silent waiters . . . white satin guerrilla warriors
Sending small arrows
One
at
a
time . . .

Got us hell . . . !!!
Close the doors
Bring down the house
Hang onto your hearts
You ain't heard nothin' yet . . .
Nothing stronger in the world than people
                                      when they need to be
And nothing is as big as believing you can when you
                                      know you can't
Nothing has more prayers/more choirs/more answers/
                              more pageantry/more beauty
Than a person climbing the sky in bare feet to catch a plane
                    that has never left and may never land again

Every time I leave him
. . . It's too soon . . .
. . . And . . . Too late

XAVIER GIRL

How little I know her
. . . This convent girl
That I've become
At last . . .

Underneath
the years of paint
For all the inhabitants of me
. . . The original wood
Has been restored . . . And now

I long to be blessed
With my simple Xavier desk
My simple human form

No, not the girl with the blazing mind
Who took to legal sheets like this . . .
Not the raging girl
Who planned to murder God
No,
I want only to yield to cotton sheets
Undershirts . . .
I want to abdicate my useless public names

J.P.

J.P. died with his hat on
. . . in a three piece suit
He told me that might happen
. . . "Don't let 'em get ya McGee
Put your money on your own nose kid
Play the chance . . . not the wish
Dreams are useless less they come true"
That's what he'd say . . .
A fine example . . . huh?
Princeton stardust
Beer and caviar
God knows . . .
The answers were in the questions
All along . . .

"You'll tear your pants"
That's what she'd say
And sure enough I did
Jumping fences
Stretching my backyard
All the way out into the world
In those days it was easy
. . . I was a freckle-faced warrior
Out to conquer my brother's paper route
With the safety
That I could always run down old man's alley
It was the original line
Back to my mother's arms

Well . . . I ain't saying I'm brave or nothin'
But I'm still not afraid to tear my pants
Or myself—God knows "the last sacraments

                                    repair the dreamer most"
I'll still play the chance and not the wish
And I may die from it
But I won't be in a three piece suit

SHEET MUSIC

Aren't you something to write home about?
Your eyes are full of sleep and sap
—Your night breath still caught
in the places
where babies come from—

Well—it doesn't happen often
But—it happens
all the time
Because of you
. . . I'm not afraid of morning
anymore—

I always dreamed
that I'd know a man like you
in times like these
—that your belly might fit perfectly
into the valley at the south of my back . . .

So c'mon—let your hind legs rear—
Squeeze the last of your childhood on me
Because—I'm not afraid of morning anymore—

IF I WERE A CHARLIE

If I were a Charlie . . .
And you were that cherub boy that hugged a Gracie doll
I may have seen you arc against a New York sky
Reaching blind for fly balls
When anyone with smaller dreams
Wouldn't even try . . .

If I were a Charlie
I may have seen the labored birth of all
$\qquad\qquad\qquad$ your sweet believing
I may have written you a letter
And told you that your sadness was a sacrament
(which it was)
That your great dreams would break your heart
$\qquad\qquad\qquad\qquad$ a million times
(and they will)

If I were a Charlie
I would have known that you knew all along
I may have seen you looking for your reflection
$\qquad\qquad\qquad\qquad$ in car bumpers
I may have seen you free your aunt's canary
Making up memories . . . the grandest folly of a magic child
If I were a Charlie
I would have told you then
What I know now . . .

Because it's not the man who loves my Maryskin
It's not the man who rejoices in a fire

                                        cracking its knuckles
It's not the man who keeps a skate key in his drawer
It's the boy . . . Who loved a Gracie doll
Even at the risk
Of being called a sissy . . .
It's the ten-year-old candy store Sam
That heard music before it was written
The boy who saw paintings
That were still in tubes of oil upon the shelves.

So . . . If I were a Charlie
I could have told you then . . .
That the only thing that mattered
Is that it matters now
That the only real disloyalty in life
Is denying the flight of paper airplanes

There are many things
That I cannot put on these pages
. . . Regions of human dignity
That do not come in
Common grammar . . . And

As long as people feel
There will be books like these
. . . When I'm gone
There will be further fools
Who might attempt
To write it down . . . But

All I mean to do is love you
. . . And all I mean to say
Is that I probably always will
. . . So

If you can . . . You might forgive me
For being able
To forgive you
All the time . . .

FEAR OF NOT FLYING

I'm afraid . . .
I've looked at you
And I've seen you lost
. . . I've seen the illusion
And because we have no flight pattern
No manner of travel
. . . Afraid that we might fall
I've seen us frightened on the ground . . .

I'm afraid.

I've never worked without a net before . . .
And so afraid am I to be left in the air
I stand trembling beneath you
. . .

I thought I would go to Nantucket
If you were gone . . .
I would collect gulls' eggs
And sleep with young carpenters
I would never say I loved them
Or let them stay the night
. . . I would wake up a widow in morning
I would live in metaphor
And rename the dogs

I'm afraid

But that is theater, of course
The romantic come of writers
Not my style at all
. . . I would use my pain well
As always I feared
. . . You would become a book
I would be reduced to writer
. . . People might applaud us then
Regard me as a talent
You as legend
Another . . . fair exchange

I'm afraid.

There are diving catches in life
. . . Far on the outside
Of common possibility . . .
They come in play-offs
In backyards
. . . They come

It was a wonderful weekend
No, my hair isn't long yet
But we loved each other
Just like we were afraid
We might . . .

I suppose I've had more public love
Men have married me
. . . for a lot less
Women have stayed with you
. . . for a lot more
We are grafting
Pieces of memory to form a past together
And I tell you the truth
. . . (hoping that you might love me anyway)

There are diving catches in life
. . . They come in play-offs
In backyards
. . . They come
They happen only to the very blessed
And they don't happen often
. . . But

Maybe if you still love me
When my hair is long . . .
. . . Maybe then . . .

"I LOVE YOU"

I love you . . .
I don't know how to honor us
With any less
Than plans to stay forever—
Like I said—I don't know how
To love anyone
Like this
For a while—

But sometimes
When I'm alone
When I can see
    the framework
Those larger designs
—if you will
    the Forest

It is then when I know
No matter how we promise
We are all
Leaving—

MRS. M.

Every December . . . no matter what
She'd drag out the old mufflers
And package us inside our homemade caps
And every hurt healed
Every problem dissolved
In white forgiving
And . . . like kittens
We snuggled in against her
As she licked us clean of everything but love

Every December . . . no matter what
We'd find our way home from schools and lovers
Leave the world's promises
For a pumpkin pie
And every hunger fed
By the safety of that lady's smile
Christmas was our membership home

Every December . . . no matter what
With Holiday confetti on my floors
I look at the cranberry stains on my hands
A sure sign that I'm carrier of love
And I pass the seeds along to Molly . . . And
All the clocks turn back to home
Where they began

22068 PACIFIC COAST HIGHWAY

I am home . . .
. . . I am
Here in this shy white cottage
Among the accidental giants
The architects fancy
I will not go up for auction
Anymore

The ocean solves my crimes
It forgives me . . .

And you were here
Yeah you were . . . All day
Hugging me like a knot
Eating life
Getting fat
Breast fed

And it was Paris in the Twenties today
With Christian painting/me at work
Michael's beauty full volume
Dropping from her bough

And I was reading O'Casey's letters
As though they were our own
Written . . . By you and me
I was that connected
You were here today

And who is this dancing girl
Who runs to the pier
Like a tourist
Autographed by strangers' smiles
Who is this dancing girl?

I'm not saying that it will always
Be . . . like this
But surely there will be other days
Like this . . .
When only you
Will be enough

And someday I will build a dam
Hold back my life for just that time
I will bring you here
Pleasure you
Keep you by letting you go
And you will be home
Not forever
But now and then
Like me

THE BOY FROM PROVINCETOWN

I can only hope that you'll remember
The print on the fabric . . .
. . . the loud rumblings of your stomach
And how you quickly
Cleaned your fingernails
With the crease of the
Matchbook cover . . .
Because I've never seen
A trembling
Like yours . . .
. . . I always hoped you would think
About that later
. . . when you could cry
And when you understood the testimony
Of the skin . . .

Your face was just
Five years younger than mine . . .
Yet the infancy of it . . .
Your boy teeth
. . . the dents where braces must have been
The way you didn't appreciate your Mother
. . . or think you ever would . . .
I could only hope that you would know
The importance of gooseflesh . . . and
That asking . . .

And I prayed that you came
To make memories
. . . not love
That I might be the lady
You tell your wife about . . .
. . . or think of when you're playing
With your children
In later Provincetown summers

Because you came to me
With no more than a perfect ass
. . . A new driver
And however awesome the machine
You didn't handle it well
. . . For all the checking you did
Under your armpits
. . . The failure wasn't in your glands . . .

It is not that you wore too much cologne
. . . You were a boy
And boys always wear too much cologne
Chew three sticks of gum at once
. . . Sex is often junk food
And sportfucking is a critical exam . . .

I had hoped that you'd remember
The cry of the gulls . . .
The flowers we left in the sink
. . . the Trinity shorts

Of your Baptism . . .
Because I've never seen a trembling
Like yours . . . and
How could I have known
. . . That after all
The innocence was mine . . .

ANTIQUES

The old clocks
Can teach us a lot . . .
. . . we can be wise
With the ticking
Of the dead hands'
Craftsmanship . . .
. . . We can overpay for
The dead woman's quilt . . .

And we could write essays now
Of then . . .
And read
Them later . . . But
Isn't admiration of the dead
A safe competition?
Are these sensitivities always
Testament to character . . . ? And

. . . Are we Romantics
Any less a group
Than the
Knights of Columbus?

FOR CHRISTIAN
–WHO HAS NO ADDRESS ANYMORE

For Christian . . . who has no address anymore . . .
                                    who accompanies the
wild geese with his violins . . . above the bay . . .
                                    above the bay . . .

And yes there are things I've always wanted
                                    that I'll never have . . .
I'll probably never play a guitar . . . sing my own songs
I don't think I'll ever wear out a pair
                                    of ballet slippers
Or
Have a son . . .
But on my floors in the middle of the night
I find raw chords and dance with native Mozarts
And there was MICHAEL
. . . For a while . . .

I thought about what you said to me
Not only what the words meant . . . But more
What the words meant coming from you . . .
The freedom heart
. . . The dream eater . . .

I do love more than one of you
In different ways at different times
And it may be that I'm too friendly to be a friend . . .

But people don't leave me just 'cause they leave . . .
And you've been hurt . . . I'm sure
More by lovers than friends I suspect
And more then than now . . .
And I think you would rather this kind of going
When it comes . . .
Not to be easily taken . . .

Not to fall from the sky politely into the sea
But to die living
To be born to death
. . . Christian
There are things I've always wanted that I'll never have . . .
But on my floors in the middle of the night
You can hear me rustle my pages
Flapping all my wings against the air
Tearing through the conversations . . . beating away
                                            The wild geese
Playing my violin . . . above the bay . . . above the bay . . .

BATTLE HIM

We don't know each other very well
And I suspect we never will
Still . . .
We have a powerful effect on each other's lives
We are on each other's minds
And we lie permanently in each other's stomachs—And
That's the truth
. . . It may be more important for me to say it
Than it is for you to hear it . . .
. . . But
It wasn't me that took him
Or you that lost him . . .

It was him
All along.

FOR THE WOMAN
WHO WANTED TO KNOW WHY . . .

First of all . . . You *know* why
And you know that men are taken
By time
Not by other women . . .

So if she's been loved by your husbands,
                                              your fathers and your sons
You already know . . .
That she never forced their mouths to breathe affection
She never took them screaming to her breast
She never raped and ripped their clothes that fall carelessly
                                              on the hardwood floors
Beside her bed . . .
She did open the doors they knocked upon . . . like you did
But . . . The rest of it they did themselves . . .

So don't ask why . . .
You *know* why . . .
It happens because of hunger . . . real or imagined
It's a natural prayer
. . . The body sends a fierce invitation
And it happens sometimes
Just because
It does . . .

And she's sorry . . . she is really . . .
Not sorry that it happened

But sorry that it hurt you . . .
And she will always be profoundly sad
That people do that to each other

I'm sure we'll never be old enough
To understand it all . . .
But I promise you
The very things you see and love about someone
Can be seen and loved by someone else . . .
And she never demanded that their bodies beg for more
She never forced them to love her or lie to you . . . But
She did open the doors they knocked upon . . . like you
The rest they did themselves . . .

FOR THE GIRLS
WHO PARK ON THE BACK LOT . . .

She was born to be comfortable with holy men/
                              the permission machines
To bring ginseng tea to the creative Jesus/
                              the deciders/
To anticipate the hunt/to protect the corporate jewels
Saddle up the fastest horse/No she never learned to ride
She was born to an unrecorded aristocracy/
                              the true queen that never reigned
She is among the voices who answer the phones
Among the cars who yield
Among the footnotes
In his biography.

She is here to fence his talent
Close it behind private doors
Cover up the holes
Protect him from the mirrors
That magnify
His warts.

And she is here to pay your respects
And his . . .
She was born to represent Gods
This female priest
Who gives you his communion
While he curses you
And sleeps.

She was born to be comfortable with holy men
To throw her body down
To be the anonymous fly in the ointment
To keep you from getting the number
Of his private line
Which is, of course
Her own.

Among the anonymous callers
Among the common denominators
Among the flock of sheep
Undetectable . . . except for the key
                                that hangs around her neck
She is the only road/the only guard
                                who can get you through
She is the treasurer of his attention
So get to know her name gentleman
She could arrange for you to be forgotten
As easily as you've forgotten her . . .

HENRY

What a lousy Emerson I'd make Henry
. . . disguised as a poet
Who dabbles in philosophy
And makes movies on the side . . . C'mon . . .

I always thought that you were more
The southernmost thinker . . .
Leaving doors and weekends open
. . . forging memories
To fit what you remembered. . . .
What a lousy Emerson you would make Henry . . .
. . . disguised as a writer
Who dabbles in poetry
And paints pictures on the side . . .

Perhaps I am not the ordinary Columbus
. . . But surely I'm a tourist just the same
And you must know how all your explorations
Built roads through land uncharted still
By Emersons and Whitmans . . .
You didn't limit yourself to interstate highways
Or logic . . . No . . .
You went beneath the Earth and hit the nerves
. . . You are a steal at $3.98 Miller . . .
The rarest of gifts . . .

And they may rejoice in all your work
And call you writer . . . of the highest kind—

The southernmost poet who paints pictures on the side . . .
But more than that . . .
You've been an Archaeologist . . .
Excavating on your hands and knees
. . . it was you who drew the maps . . . disguised as words
You . . . who could spot the pilgrim soul a mile away
. . . Because of you . . . We are closer to ourselves

C'mon . . .
You've caught me doing it again . . .
What a lousy Emerson I'd make Henry . . .
Forging poetry like this
With my bare hearts
. . . a cheap shot I'd say
For a girl to share the page with you and Walt . . .
                              and Ralph Waldo . . .
As though the bunch of us were pals . . .
C'mon . . .

. . . Even at the risk that I might take this
                              all too seriously
Close to Christmas like this . . . Irish fool
                              that I am this time of year . . .
I only came to say this much . . .
That you've been the rarest of gifts . . .
A grand inheritance
A hooligan who worked for scale

A funny Valentine
An original sin

154

An Eastern Santa Claus
And because finally it matters
. . . You are the most splendid of men
A woman's feast
The rarest of gifts. . . .

FOR THE LADY DOCTOR
ON THE FIRST FLOOR RIGHT . . .

High speed I called you
. . . accelerated
First class wisdom
. . . an institution arrow
Heart surgeon
In Wednesday clothes . . .

In coming there
. . . I found a cure
While you
Found a further disease
. . .

Bless the malfunctions
That plague the body and its mind
. . . Without them medicine would be subsidized drilling
And the economy of doctors
Lost . . . Oh
Bless these problems
For the doctor's sake . . .

Our pain is product . . .
. . . It is

And you explore the tissue
in payment
For payment . . .

And you lost me on the table
. . . I was awake
You didn't like that . . .

I found a cure
. . . Insulted by that inconvenience
You were a credit to your profession
. . . You found
A further disease . . .

And you *are* extraordinary
. . . Dangerous . . . if you wish
Because pain is your product
. . . your mean
And similar
Touché

RETROSPECTIVE

It's the prayer of every hitchhiker
I think . . .
"Please don't make
                          Freedom a sin . . ."

I don't think about it very often
But . . . I always thought that someday
I would put out my thumb
Tear off my silks
And ride . . .

But outlaws
Don't have the eyes of a doe
The trembling heart of a sparrow
Besides . . . I used my courage
And . . . I only have
A few time-outs left . . . But

I still think about the wind
In my hair . . .
The wildflowers on Old Forbes Road
The music of my army boots
on Laurel Mountain
The night I ran away from home
Forever . . .

Even at its price of pain . . .
The rush of sad songs it later wrote
Not only would I do it all again
. . . I wouldn't even ask
To be fifteen . . .

CORRESPONDENCE

"Malloy, you must be in love"
"Me . . . In Love . . . You Turkey bookseller . . . You
                                    Yalie love peddler . . . You
three-pieced double-breasted feeling eater . . ."

"I love it Malloy . . . You're writing again . . . You hate
                                    that you love it"

"Listen you tight-assed Communist ring kisser . . . You're
                                    not gonna sell
My love on pages . . . Edit MY life with your erasers . . .
                                    You flat-eyed hypocrite . . .
I don't want to be your vision"

"Malloy . . . Malloy . . . You crazy red gypsy lady . . . Go
                                    ahead and let me have it . . .
But send me the pages, will ya?"

"Send you the pages, huh? . . . You gravedigger . . . You
                                    Gucci wasp tease . . .
You Connecticut Train pimp . . . Yeah . . . I do hate that
                                    I love it . . . You
Nazi poet coach . . ."

            The pages went out today
            Full of you
            Full of me . . .

Smeared and arrived . . .
We are in the mail
Going toward a Yalie love peddler
Carrying us back to New York
To publish us forever . . .
We are translated into words for now
Wasted on strangers
. . . I'm sorry

THOSE FIRST CLOSETS

Remember when you were Superman
And I was Lois Lane??
. . . Yeah . . .
Everything you said had importance
. . . I was amazed by the sight of your razor
On my sink those first mornings . . .
And the size of your shoes
. . . The way they seemed to protect mine
In those first closets
. . . And our name on the mailbox . . . Oh
They were splendid times. . . .

The first time I signed your name
And made it mine . . .
When the gas man called me Mrs.
. . . When my Mother introduced you to Jack
As my husband . . . Oh
All my dolls died that day . . .
My childhood was forgiven
Your presence was restitution
For all the beer I stole from the basement
. . . Your choice of me
Made good all my adolescent testimony
. . . Your love
Was a full pardon
Your ring gave me membership
To the good china
. . . Because of you

I was finally one of them
. . . Yeah . . .

And didn't my brother open the car doors for me
When I was pregnant? . . . Oh
That baby earned me respect
. . . I was holy then
Even your Father cried
. . . Let me drive the new car first
And when the baby called me 'Mama'
I couldn't let her go
. . . That word renamed me
Made all my nicknames silly
. . . Yeah

We were something then
. . . When you were the young Lincoln
And I was all those faithful girls at home
I've been cynical about it since . . . And yes
The years have changed my pleasures many times . . . But
I'll never be too sophisticated to forget
That the wearing of your wedding ring stopped me
                                        from biting my nails
For all my flights . . . I still recall the days
When I was all grown-up . . . When
I passed for white
. . . Earned my passage
Yeah . . .

No matter
what they tell you
. . . it is always today

THE DEAL MAKER

So this is the way it happens
. . . You find yourself playing with babies
In grocery lines
. . . You're tempted to buy flowers
From the kids who wait at the freeway entrances
. . . Rocking horses have an almost religious charm
You finally hear the words to songs and
. . . That's it . . .
Pretty soon you start wondering again if there really

is a God

. . . And if he might remember you
And make this deal . . .
You promise him five years as a missionary in the jungle

If only

He would make your new boyfriend call (in the

next 5 minutes)

. . . Half hour?

You find yourself at 3 A.M.
Searching the bookshelf for the old astrology manual
. . . If the manual doesn't agree with your obsession
Your mind tricks you into remembering

That you were a week premature

And should have been born on the cusp . . .
If anyone knew what you were really thinking . . .

(Especially HIM)

. . . You would be put in protective custody
By the authorities . . . (Remember them?)

And it gets worse . . .
. . . You start leaving all your make-up on
                                        When you sleep with him
Your skin objects by producing large bumps and
Increasing its pores—So

You put on more make-up . . .
. . . You brush your teeth sixty times a day . . .
You chew whole packs of gum and
While everybody else on the road is looking at the road
You're dangerously checking your lip gloss
                                        in the rearview mirror . . .
. . . At a stoplight . . . EVERY TIME
Somebody has to honk you back to reality . . .
. . . Nobody would ever believe it
Nobody. . . .

THE NUTCRACKER

I was nine
The first time I saw the 'Nutcracker'
. . . And it stayed in my eyes
They were six years old
. . . Little white ice cream cone girls
Were they born perfect
. . . All their homework done
Born pink?
. . . How did they get so wonderful
In six years?

It took me a year (twice a week)
Just to learn the five positions
. . . And nine years old
Is far too late
To be wonderful
At six.

MESSAGES

I thought about your dream
. . . The romance of it
The racism of it
How your mind segregated the characters
. . . Us and
Them . . .
The good guys and
The bad guys . . .

I don't really think that the scenes will come true
. . . Certainly not as you dreamed
That was your mind's trick . . . But
I can see us on our knees
. . . I can see us tremble as the eagle's arm reach out
Across the ceiling of the skies
. . . Believe can make you tremble
You can laugh
. . . But the blind have seen before

There are small magicians in the mind
. . . They perform beneath the eyes when we're asleep
And all of them are messengers
All of them . . .
Difficult to translate
. . . harder still to even remember
But

I thought about your dream
. . . how you saw those early months as calvary
Knowing we entered the innocent snow
Assured at resurrection . . .
That exception bestowed on just you and me alone
. . . *The absolute right*
To be wrong . . .

Now you can laugh if you want
. . . But that's one hell
of a message . . .

ACKNOWLEDGMENTS

Little known feelings and facts that mean different things at different times for different reasons . . . and sometimes not for any reason at all . . .

First of all . . . Licorice is a wonderful thing and
Before I forget . . .
I'm grateful to the people or persons
                                    who invented Ko-rec-type . . .
I will always admire the simple grace of
                                    Art Garfunkel's voice
. . . I wish I were an old friend of Lillian Hellman's
I think a lot about the design in store windows and
                                    appreciate the art . . .
I like the feel of fine wood—of craftsmanship . . .
I think sheepdogs are perverse . . . have a mad whimsy . . .
                                    I like the
underside of their paws . . . I like the polka dots
                                    on their bellies . . .
I think Burgess Meredith has beautiful eyes . . .
I wonder about hummingbirds . . . occasionally . . .
I understand every word that Diane Keaton says . . .
                                    and I like her
. . . I have never kissed anyone under the Bridge of Sighs
I eat orange rinds . . .
I just found out there was a Manzanar . . . and that
Vitamins have calories . . .
. . . Hershey bars always taste the same . . .
                                    no matter what

I took the money out of my collection envelope at St. Pius at
                                                    least twice a month
And buried it under the spruce tree in the yard . . .
. . . I think all cats are female
I appreciate John Denver/Joan Dideon and
. . . I will never forget the Act of Contrition . . .
I am always amazed to see someone play the piano or
                                          type without looking . . .
. . . Daylight Savings Time delights me . . .
I wonder . . . why the manufacturers of vibrators warn us
against using them for unexplained calf pains . . .
I have ripped off all those tags that I could not rip off
                                          under penalty of law . . .
. . . I love the smell of gasoline and
I have never been able to allow a cake to cool sufficiently
                                          before eating it . . .
Finally
. . . I have never looked for J. D. Salinger (although
                                          I've thought about it)
I miss those small boxes that Sen-Sens used to
                                          come in . . . and
One last thought . . . (keep in mind that it comes from a
                                          girl who steals
towels from the same hotels where she checks the
                                          drawer for Bibles)
. . . I've often wondered if it's not so much what we
                                          believe that matters
But only IF we believe . . .
I'm never tempted to ask for whom the bell tolls
. . . In my last breaths . . . I'll be just as charming as ever

I'll argue that these pages were prayers
. . . That Ann Sexton paid too high a price for the Pulitzer
                                              and that God

let me back in an unmarked car . . .

(If you know Laurence Olivier—will you just put your
                                       arms around him . . .
Nah . . . you don't have to say anything . . .)

ABOUT THE AUTHOR

I was born in the morning of my first year.
My Mother and Father loved me like a rock.
Some say they felt that maybe I was broken
That life would deal me one last card
Well . . . It didn't
And I'm not . . .
I'm not . . .

My Father was a lover . . . A dandy . . . A good old boy—
He was brought to a desk at thirty-seven
He died within a year
His paintings not yet dry . . .
And my Mother had a tragic beauty
And when it left it took her with it
Even though it never left . . .
Change sometimes looks like death . . .
"Oh, to ruin the afternoon longing for the morning Mama
To lose the evening for the afternoon . . ."
She wasn't always with me
. . . But she was always with me . . .

Charlie gave me dreams too big for little girls . . .
Even now they hardly fit . . .
And watching her die wasn't easy . . . knowing
                                        she wanted to . . .
"Mary . . ." the note began . . . "Can you forgive me please
. . . It's the last thing I'll need . . . The last thing I'll ask
. . . Oh Mary . . . Can you release me please?"

She died the same year Bobby died . . . The
                                    year of Mac . . .
                           The year of leaving
. . . I was twenty-one . . .

I lived most of my life in Bethlehem, Pennsylvania
In a grand brick house . . . Lots of willow
                                    trees and yes . . .
The long rope swing . . .
I had a dog named Buttons and Bows and my brothers were
In the Little League . . .
I had a balcony and a white eyelet bedspread
Everyone wanted to be me . . . Even me . . .

My grandfather lived in the great gray house
                      above the boulevard . . . With Gracie
The priests had dinner there every Monday night
And . . . So did I . . .
They brought me tiny rosary beads
And never kissed me on the lips . . .

My Mother took a pill they say
And made us born like this . . .
But hell . . . We used to think and say
"What's wrong with born like this?"

And we had an ocean house his last summer
Salty maple bunk beds/oilcloth breakfast/
                                    the family pageants
How was I to know it could have ended?

176

The table set for twenty-five
(Cecelia never married)
And I believed in God so hard
I prayed out loud two times
So he could hear me . . .

HE left on a Tuesday . . .
Didn't even say Good-bye
And we all fell apart like toys
Broken . . . And no one to play with us anymore.
Nothing was ever the same again
Peter locked himself in the bathroom . . .
                                        (Still can't talk about it)
Tally went to the seminary
I went begging for some comfort
But . . . All my mother's milk was dry

And I was lost in the crowds in the kitchen
. . . How could bedtime be at eight
The night your Father dies?

After that I was careful not to love anything too much
Not me . . . I knew what dead meant
And no one rocked it away
I was alone . . . I knew that much . . .
And it was going to be that way for the rest of my life
. . . Or so I thought at seven . . .
I decided not to talk all summer . . . And I didn't
I wrote letters to God in those great big
                                        second grade letters

And when he didn't answer
. . . Not a word
I decided never to write to him ever again
And except for holidays . . . and when Mac was born
I never have. . . .

"There comes a time"
 Dylan sings
"When we gotta serve somebody"

I won't suggest that I know *exactly* what he means
(although the songs he writes for Jesus

                                        are just as powerful
as the songs he wrote when he loved Sarah . . .) . . . But

There does come a time
When we've lived long enough to know
That there is room for everything
To happen twice . . .
. . . A time when we can love two people at the same time
And we choose to love one of them
More . . .

I don't expect that you could use my memory
. . . or his
And I won't pretend that you didn't pay good money
For this book . . .
Or that Dylan didn't profit from the war . . .
. . . Tradition is not going to end here
And I would be a liar if I thought
This was literature . . . Or
That I could teach you anything
. . . I can't . . . But, I suspect

There comes a time in every woman
When she allows herself

The comfort of her own breasts . . .
. . . When she understands blood
A time when she is no longer an immigrant
In a man's arms . . .

That time has come for me
I'll take it in the vein
. . . Beware